WILD ANIMALS

LEATHERBACK SEA TURTLES

BY DALTON RAINS

WWW.APEXEDITIONS.COM

Copyright © 2026 by Apex Editions, Mendota Heights, MN 55120. All rights reserved. No part of this book may be reproduced or utilized in any form or by any means without written permission from the publisher.

Apex is distributed by North Star Editions:
sales@northstareditions.com | 888-417-0195

Produced for Apex by Red Line Editorial.

Photographs ©: Shutterstock Images, cover, 1, 4–5, 6–7, 8, 9, 14, 15, 16–17, 22–23, 24, 26–27, 29; Julien Renoult/iNaturalist, 10–11; Chris Quirin/iNaturalist, 12–13, 25; Wildestanimal/Moment/Getty Images, 18–19, 20, 21

Library of Congress Control Number: 2025930916

ISBN
979-8-89250-549-9 (hardcover)
979-8-89250-585-7 (paperback)
979-8-89250-653-3 (ebook pdf)
979-8-89250-621-2 (hosted ebook)

Printed in the United States of America
Mankato, MN
082025

NOTE TO PARENTS AND EDUCATORS

Apex books are designed to build literacy skills in striving readers. Exciting, high-interest content attracts and holds readers' attention. The text is carefully leveled to allow students to achieve success quickly. Additional features, such as bolded glossary words for difficult terms, help build comprehension.

TABLE OF CONTENTS

CHAPTER 1
TO THE OCEAN 4

CHAPTER 2
BIG BODIES 10

CHAPTER 3
EAT UP 16

CHAPTER 4
LIFE CYCLE 22

COMPREHENSION QUESTIONS • 28
GLOSSARY • 30
TO LEARN MORE • 31
ABOUT THE AUTHOR • 31
INDEX • 32

CHAPTER 1

TO THE OCEAN

Ocean waves crash over an empty beach. Suddenly, the sand moves. A tiny flipper appears. Then a small nose pops out. It's a baby leatherback sea turtle.

Baby sea turtles must dig through about 2 feet (0.6 m) of sand to get out of their nests.

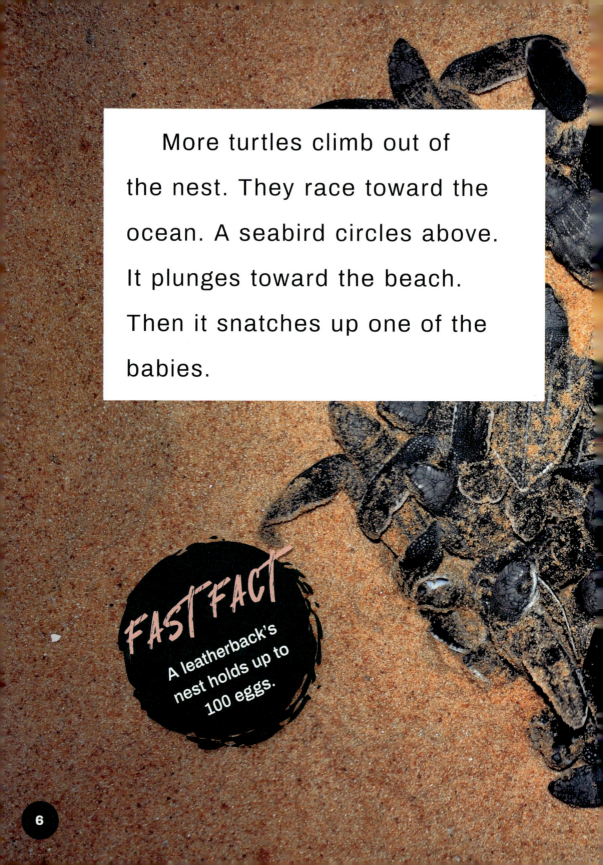

More turtles climb out of the nest. They race toward the ocean. A seabird circles above. It plunges toward the beach. Then it snatches up one of the babies.

FAST FACT
A leatherback's nest holds up to 100 eggs.

All the sea turtles in a nest leave at the same time.

Leatherbacks usually hatch at night. They use moonlight to find the ocean.

There are too many turtles for the bird to catch. Many of the babies reach the ocean. They begin their lives at sea.

STAYING ALIVE

About 1 in 1,000 leatherback hatchlings lives to adulthood. Eggs and hatchlings may be eaten by birds, crabs, or other animals. Or humans may collect the eggs for food.

Baby leatherbacks live on their own right away.

CHAPTER 2

BIG BODIES

Leatherback sea turtles are the world's largest turtles. A single leatherback may weigh 2,000 pounds (900 kg) or more.

Adult leatherbacks are about 7 feet (2.1 m) long from head to tail.

Unlike other turtles, a leatherback does not have a hard shell outside its body. Instead, it has a **flexible** covering. A layer of tiny connected bones is underneath the tough skin.

FAST FACT
A leatherback's soft shell can **contract**. A harder shell would crack in deep water.

Leatherbacks' skin feels like leather. That's what the turtles are named after.

A leatherback's front flippers spread up to 9 feet (2.7 m) wide.

Leatherbacks use their huge front flippers to move through the water. Their rear flippers are smaller. These paddle-shaped flippers help with **steering**.

DEEP DIVERS

Leatherbacks can swim faster and deeper than any other **reptile**. They can swim as fast as 22 miles per hour (35 km/h). And they can dive 4,200 feet (1,280 m) deep.

Leatherbacks can stay underwater for up to 85 minutes.

CHAPTER 3

EAT UP

Leatherback sea turtles live in the Atlantic, Pacific, and Indian Oceans. Adults travel as far north as Canada and Norway. The turtles can be found as far south as New Zealand.

Leatherbacks live in more places around the world than any other reptile.

FAST FACT
A thick layer of fat keeps heat inside a leatherback's body.

A leatherback's flippers warm up when they move. Then, warm blood moves to the turtle's body.

Leatherbacks often dive for food. Unlike other reptiles, they can stay warm in cold water. That lets the turtles survive in the chilly deep sea.

A leatherback eats almost three-quarters of its weight in food every day.

Leatherbacks are **omnivores**. The turtles mostly eat **prey** with soft bodies. Jellyfish are a common meal. The turtles also eat crabs, fish, and seaweed.

MOUTHPARTS

A leatherback has a pointy **jaw**. Spines cover the inside of the turtle's mouth and throat. The spines point backward. That keeps prey inside the leatherback's mouth.

The spines in a leatherback's mouth are called papillae.

CHAPTER 4

LIFE CYCLE

Leatherbacks **mate** every two to four years. The turtles migrate between feeding areas and nesting areas. These areas are usually about 3,700 miles (6,000 km) apart.

Some leatherbacks travel more than 10,000 miles (16,000 km) every year.

Leatherbacks mate and nest between February and July.

After mating, a female swims to shore. She lays many eggs and buries them in the sand. A female builds several nests in a single nesting season.

FAST FACT
Male leatherbacks spend their entire lives at sea. Females leave the water only to lay eggs.

Baby leatherbacks weigh less than 3 ounces (85 g).

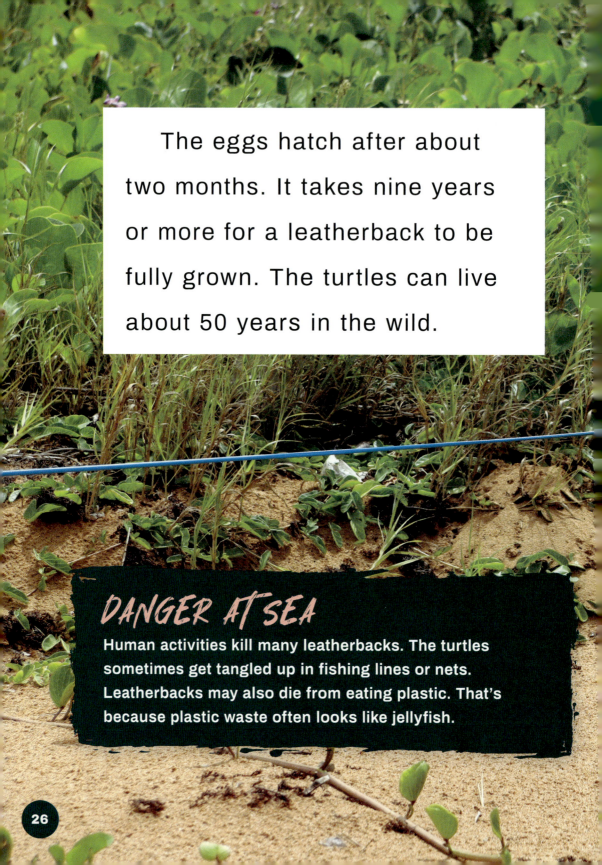

The eggs hatch after about two months. It takes nine years or more for a leatherback to be fully grown. The turtles can live about 50 years in the wild.

DANGER AT SEA

Human activities kill many leatherbacks. The turtles sometimes get tangled up in fishing lines or nets. Leatherbacks may also die from eating plastic. That's because plastic waste often looks like jellyfish.

Some beaches are protected. That gives leatherbacks a safe place to lay eggs.

COMPREHENSION QUESTIONS

Write your answers on a separate piece of paper.

1. Write a few sentences explaining the main ideas of Chapter 3.

2. Which feature of leatherback sea turtles do you find most interesting? Why?

3. How deep can a leatherback sea turtle dive?
   - A. 7 feet (2.1 m)
   - B. 4,200 feet (1,280 m)
   - C. 22 miles (35 km)

4. Why do leatherback sea turtles lay so many eggs?
   - A. so that the baby sea turtles can eat one another
   - B. so that predators will eat all the eggs and babies
   - C. so the eggs and babies will not all get eaten

5. What does **plunges** mean in this book?

*A seabird circles above. It **plunges** toward the beach. Then it snatches up one of the babies.*

    A. moves downward
    B. moves upward
    C. stays still

6. What does **migrate** mean in this book?

*The turtles **migrate** between feeding areas and nesting areas. These areas are usually about 3,700 miles (6,000 km) apart.*

    A. to dive straight down
    B. to stay in one place forever
    C. to move from one part of the world to another

Answer key on page 32.

GLOSSARY

contract
To become smaller.

flexible
Able to bend without breaking.

jaw
One of the two bones that form an animal's mouth.

mate
To form a pair and come together to have babies.

omnivores
Animals that eat both plants and animals.

prey
Animals that are hunted and eaten by other animals.

reptile
An animal that has scales and a backbone.

steering
Controlling the direction something moves.

BOOKS

Donnelly, Rebecca. *On the Move with Leatherback Sea Turtles*. Jump!, 2023.

Hutter, Carollyne. *Reptile Migration*. Focus Readers, 2024.

Norton, Elisabeth. *Deepest Divers.* Apex Editions, 2023.

ONLINE RESOURCES

Visit **www.apexeditions.com** to find links and resources related to this title.

ABOUT THE AUTHOR

Dalton Rains is an author and editor from Saint Paul, Minnesota.

B
beach, 4, 6

D
dive, 15, 19

E
eggs, 6, 9, 24–26

F
flippers, 4, 14

H
hatchlings, 9

J
jaw, 21
jellyfish, 20, 26

M
mate, 22, 24
migrate, 22

N
nest, 6, 22, 24

O
oceans, 4, 6, 8, 16
omnivores, 20

P
prey, 20–21

S
shell, 12–13

ANSWER KEY:
1. Answers will vary; 2. Answers will vary; 3. B; 4. C; 5. A; 6. C